SELVAGE

Selvage

Donna Johnson

Carnegie Mellon University Press
Pittsburgh 2013

Acknowledgments

Grateful acknowledgments to the editors of these journals, in which the following poems originally appeared:

Birmingham Poetry Review: "Passional"; *Café Review*: "The Enslaved Sister of My Imagination"; *Cutbank*: "Einarsson" (winner, 2010 Cutbank Online Contest); *Del Sol Review*: "Cinderella," "Déjeuner sur l'herbe," "The brief occasion of my father's happiness"; *Green Mountains Review*: "Bell's Palsy," "Peine forte et dure"; *Ibbetson Street Magazine*: "From Stars"; *Marco Polo*: "On Being Mistaken for a Whore in a Laundromat, Pensacola[,] Florida, July 12, 1979"; *Oracle Literary Review*: "Subtext of the Latest Rejection"; *Perihelion*: "Portrait of the Artist as a Twelve Year Old"; *Poetry Porch*: "Bee Balm"; *Roanoke Review*: "Wait"; *Two Rivers Review*: "Anniversary" (Honorable Mention, 2002 Two Rivers Poetry Prize), "The Summer You Told Me I Was Beautiful"; University of Nevada at Reno, Black Rock Press: "Heirloom" (winner, 1999 Broadside Competition)

I am deeply grateful for the guidance and knowledge of past teachers, including Pamela Anderson, Daniel Bosch, Catherine Bowman, Lucie Brock-Broido, Henri Cole, Joan Houlihan, and Pamela Bailey Powers, as well as to friends and fellow poets from past workshops in Cambridge and Concord who have shared with me their encouragement, wisdom, and love of poetry. Also, a special thanks to Kim Triedman and Joanne Reynolds, who helped me work through several versions of this manuscript.

Book design by Leslie Sainz

Library of Congress Control Number 2012938306
ISBN 978-0-88748-562-6
Copyright © by Donna Johnson
All rights reserved
Printed and bound in the United States of America
10 9 8 7 6 5 4 3 2 1

for Sam,
Mia and Sophie

Contents

I. Dogwood Winter

The Enslaved Sister of My Imagination	15
The brief occasion of my father's happiness	17
Portrait of the Artist as a Twelve Year Old	18
Notions	20
Photograph of My Father at Six	21
Stephens, Georgia	22
Wait	24
The Children of Sheriff Wilfred Hunnington Speak	25
White	27
Tennessee Walker	28
Cousin Jesse's Annual Checkup	29
Eve Gets a Makeover	31
Streptococcus Pneumoniae	32
Yellow Is the Color of West Texas	33
Field Trip to Andrew Jackson's Hermitage, 1969	34
Heirloom	35
Dogwood Winter	37

II. Selvage

On being mistaken for a whore in a laundromat, Pensacola Florida, July 12, 1979	41
The Summer You Told Me I Was Beautiful	42
Einarsson	43
Cinderella	45

Bell's Palsy	46
Paean to the Opiate	47
Déjeuner sur l'herbe	49
The More Dangerous Amusement	50
Chew	52
Liver's Retort	53
She Dreams of Four Ways Around Her Dilemma	54
Other Means Having Failed	56
Ritual	57
Selvage	59

III. Passional

Peine forte et dure	63
Che gelida manina	64
Cave	65
The Plot in North Village	67
Anniversary	68
Promise, No Pinky Cross	70
I have no ideas, but I do have some things	72
Kneeling Under Sky, Against Which, The Clouds	74
Cosmology	75
Subtext of the Latest Rejection	76
Michelangelo's Eves	78
Antiphon	80
Locus	81
Lazarus	83

Cassandra at Dinner	84
Relations	85
Anniversary	86
Passional	87
Bee Balm	88
From stars	89
The Child in Wonder Falling on Grass	91
Notes	93

I love all waste
And solitary places; where we taste
The pleasure of believing what we see . . .

—Percy Bysshe Shelley, "Julian and Maddalo"

I. Dogwood Winter

The Enslaved Sister of My Imagination

Years of the new math did me no good against her.
Her wrists sprout blackberry vines and chicory
and she calls herself *Her Most High*. She calls herself
*Sister Mary Margaret Katherine Anne
of the Order of the Shit Eating Grinners.*
She says, "But you can call me Sister."

She distracts me in the houseofthelord. She bet me
that the gigantic stock boy with the black eyes
could put his thumb down my pants and each finger
between the buttons of my shirt without popping a one.

She tries to appease me, whispers Latin nouns in my ear,
in my favorite case, the ablative. If I say "rosa,"
she says "elephantine." If I say "alms and tutelage,"
she says "cherry ice." She seeks out the most interminable
and joyous of all mysteries in beds of salvia
and nests of stinging ants. She takes me
by the shoulders and holds me until I start to weep.
I despise this most about her.

She brings mice. The last one still had one of its eyes.
Tiny, black, and mesmerizing as a poppy seed.
And she thinks it moves me that in June braided heads
of red clover weave through the pennyroyal.

I'd rather be an archangel of pitch pine, a brown-legged girl
from the Church of the Nazarene in white batiste
who nightsweats Dutch and Hindi throughout the entirety
of Pentecost. I'd rather my chin wart and pinch like a crone's,
than let her back into my house again.

Let me know if you ever see that girl around here, 'cause
I'll send her white basket of lilies packing; I'll send
her so far down that lunged fish will devour all
but the spiders that once laced her heart.

The brief occasion of my father's happiness

occurred somewhere between Texarkana
and Wichita Falls. Back home, the Bermuda grass
was being mowed by a twelve year old;

the new pumps my mother had bought
were still hidden in the bedroom closet
and the bill lay unopened in the mailbox.

At the Howard Johnson's we swam through
the lights of a heated swimming pool.
We ate powdered donuts, lying five to a bed.

The Impala had not yet overheated, my father's
father had not yet teetered on the step stool to take
the tawny port from the highest shelf.

While we slept in the back seat, my mother looked up,
following the shadow of a single cloud as it turned
a portion of wheat field from gold to brown.

Portrait of the Artist as a Twelve Year Old

I'm a slick of feeling, half eel, half child,
a muslin invalid with a pinup's smile.
A dust bowl of sulk in my every wake,
I'm a name-caller, door-slammer,
skidder from grace. What I touch,
I neither fix, nor break.

I squirrel ribbons and buttons,
paperbacks with yellowed pages.
There's always a mess trailing
from my velvet satchels.
When the neighbor boys catch
a whiff, they follow.

Mama's at a loss. Hews petticoats
from shrimp net and lace,
sews bells in the hems,
so I can't get away. But my secrets
go unwashed, knees rough as hickory bark.
My voice is part cottonmouth; the other part, lark.

When I can't abide the stale blue of my walls,
I run back into the woods, skirt
the shale of the creek's dry summer bed,
where lone, and out of earshot
of the house's reproach, I prick my thumb,
pluck berries from a wolfwillow bush.

I make a black tea to quarter the moon,
keep me new as a quail's egg, feral and smooth.
But I turn wasp-waisted, bud scarlet and plagued,
my tongue, a clamp, my heart's heart, vague.

Notions

for Della

Your mother had notions. Wouldn't buy Ivory soap—
not because she saw the irony, that whiteness
equals purity, not because it reminded her
of all the carved tusks looted from Abidjan ruins
curled around the wrists of Belle Meade denizens—
she thought it smelled common. Cornrows
and Kente cloth were out of the question.

She clung to her book of proper, as if
it could keep one from harm: the hands of boys
inching down your pants, police slowing,
tinted windows rolling down, all because you crossed
the highway that divided the two halves of town.

She taught you to look ahead (*like you don't see nothin'*)
balancing flute case across handlebars,
approaching the house of the first clarinet,
with its lawn boy positioned at the gate,
coat and exaggerated grin, freshly painted red.

Photograph of My Father at Six

August has wrung every drop
from the foliage. Sky, a sheet
whipped by westerlies,
scorched white by the sun.

He sits next to a spiny yucca
whose flowers have withered
into hard white beads.

Brushing the house is the hackberry
he would fall from at ten. He fractured
his arm, but so successfully sopped up
his own blood that no one suspected.

It wasn't pain he feared, but being a burden:
youngest child who couldn't pull his own.
Once he'd even dreamed he went
to sell eggs and returned to find
the house deserted, furniture gone.

Even at six a bewildered sadness
tugs at the corner of his eyes.
He holds his spine overly erect,
as if it had been cured by creosote and sun,
hardened as the fence posts
that separated white town from Indian.

Stephens, Georgia

A mile from the old divided highway
that connected Atlanta to Macon
ten miles from the strip
with the McDonald's, KFC, Burger King
five miles from the strip with the
Taco Bell and KFC and

They said look for the house with the laying hens
How many of them can there be

In the heat of the day the birds
were still in the dark coop
but you could smell their smell
the decay and the life
hear music playing from a car
parked down the road

You were just shy of forty
It wasn't just the blinding migraines   the ataxia
You didn't want to leave it to chance
spontaneous thrombosis
clusters of tiny veins bursting like degenerate stars
Though the odds weren't good
you chose the surgery

You chose *Amazing Grace*
We knew most all of the verses

you knew them too, but would
also have known the author's story

The young preacher from the college town
couldn't figure why you left
or why you kept coming back

said you didn't shy from talking
about your troubles
Not meant as a compliment

and
whereas our kin are country
the fewer words the better whereas

Wait

Fumbling with the hem of a sundress, gear shift,
the smell of corn liquor and vinyl prevailing as westerlies,
you weren't out to hurt. Just following a dimestore plot:
lonely moonfaced college girl—a couple of tokes,
a quick sack. Only dusk-heavy sky, one mangy Hereford
to hear you, already unzipping, *I know you want it too.*
I tried to jerk my head sober, but cracked it
on the door handle instead. I only got out one word.
I could have been more specific. I thought words
were more substantial, could affect space, time,
but we measured time differently—your skin, already slick
as oil; mine, parched as the dryland wheat
immigrants brought from the old world, and with it,
the goathead weeds, Russian thistle, that took such hold.

The Children of Sheriff Wilfred Hunnington Speak

We knew the Man
our Father.

We knew his Hand
how it grew strong
and manifest itself
as switch and belt
and then the hewn oak limb
that he called
Brother.

We knew how the Hand
grafted to that Club
and moved with the force
of a great and massive oak.

Some call this God's Will.

But we knew how the Club
took over for the Man
when the accused ones waivered
and confessed to deeds
they could not have done
and laughed the odd
faithless laugh that only
the innocent or deranged
are capable of.

We knew how he folded
our hands gently over
each other each night.

There were prayers we said
kneeling before him
and prayers we said only to ourselves,
which, until we saw the black
dirt cast over his body
and stay upon it
unmoved, we were certain
had never been heard.

White

The goateed counselor from California
sat well-folded on the mat, asked
each student to name her favorite color.
Having a crush on him, I was grateful
to be at the far end of the circle.

I decided to choose a color before,
beyond, hue, its beauty, extreme and pure—
color of desert suns, capes of snow,
the favorite of Fitzgerald's
Daisy Buchanan.
He frowned at my answer.

Walking to the mess hall, two girls
passed each other, touched
fists lightly. *Black*, said one.
is beautiful.

Was there something in me he saw
that I could not—
Tennessee cracker, hick, bigot—

like the sound of money
in Daisy's voice—
taint that could not be
unlearned, unbred?

Tennessee Walker

There is a proper way to sit: holding your spine
perfectly straight, never slumped against the rushing
of a chair back. Always leave a little space,
just wide enough for a piece of bond to pass.

The perfect rockin' chair canter makes for smooth
ridin', always collected, an even three beats.

And a proper way to walk, as if you were a debutante
being taught how to glide across a ballroom floor,
a book, or a tea cup full of whiskey, on your head.

Pull the bit against the pink.
Don't let that filly get uppity.

There's a proper way to sing and it comes
from a place lower than you'd think.
A proper way to love.

I don't care what you heard, Mister.
We don't never sore our horses.

The room smells overwintered, of souring hay.
The filly charges, smashing the stall.
They say she's not fit to breed or show,
though when she's not under saddle,
she still has a most spectacular gait.

Cousin Jesse's Annual Checkup

I got a lazy eye and a cut on my knee
The scab turns black and I pull it off
but it come right back—howdya like that!

I got a dog. It eats Mother's flowers,
eats 'em fast and don't swallow, like Mother says
I do with French fries, and it ain't healthy.

When Doctor pokes around
something tickles and my stick goes up.
You're a little man, he says.

I put on the blue cloth. The nurse
said I got the opening wrong,
Goes in the back.

Her mouth is red, with red
wax stuck in the corners. Smells like
fruit gum. I ask for some.

My head hurts from all the thinking
Doctor wants me to do. Asks me
the name of things, shows me pictures.

One is a donkey. I tell him about
the neighbor girl's party. They put
a picture of a donkey on the wall

Me first! Me first! I say, but
Mother tugs the blindfold away.
No. Birthday girls go first.

The birthday girl is Sarah.
Ask me what color her hair is.
I can tell you. Ask. Brown.

I seen people kiss on the train.
I don't kiss the birthday girl.
She gave Terry Chambers

my Spiderman lunch box. Mother says
take it back, but he done wrote his name in it,
and now everybody thinks it's his.

Eve Gets a Makeover

I don't like to say anybody's hopeless. But, that yellow Dotted Swiss you just bought—you know, the one with the full dirndl skirt and gathered waist—makes you look wider than you are tall. Enough material in it to patch the Hindenburg. Don't fret, though hon. You got your charms. Jes' gotta make use of 'em before they're gone: a little contour cheek powder, a shade darker than your natural, some highlights. What you waitin' for? Plenty women gettin' *all* their stuff done. Who's gonna throw stones? Your kids are clean, their hair is combed. Your make cakes from scratch; once a week you bring that broccoli casserole to the nursin' home. I know what they told you. Jesus first, others second, yourself last spells J-O-Y. But joy ain't beauty. And I don't see you displayin' much of the former, anyhow, worryin' about your husband workin' late, maybe findin' someone younger. Anyway, the King James did get one thing right: all flesh is grass. That's why you best be ruthless with it. I can help you there. I know flesh. And I know ruthless.

Streptococcus Pneumoniae

Mother spoons the last of the penicillin
over vanilla ice cream, the faint smell
of plastic, molding cherries, trailing.

Coughing wracks my room;
white ribs of sunlight quake
the flowered coverlet.

When I can no longer eat a meal,
she brings Melba toast softened in ginger ale.
Holds the plate under my chin
as I cough it up.

After that, she brings water,
but it comes up too,
then watery sputum, streaked red.

The emergency room is like a kiln,
faces swirled around me
like dyes in marbleized paper:
feverish carmine and sienna.

The steel of the gurney,
the only rational thing
left in the world.

Yellow Is the Color of West Texas

Grandma claimed it was the color for whores.
The closest city to her town they named *Amarillo*,
perhaps for the clouds of Monarchs, high
on milkweed, or for homesteader's cloth,
dyed with the boiled hulls of butternut.

Each spring, coneflowers line
the interstate. Lone patches of green
sprout along irrigation pipes and ditches,
under heifer slosh from windmill barrels.
No roses bloom of their own accord,
yellow, or of any other kind.

Our family loads into the El Camino,
heads down to Palo Duro Canyon.
Grandad does not bother brushing
ocher-colored grit from ragged cracks
in aqua vinyl seats and dash. A sign greets:
REMAIN ON TRAILS, RATTLESNAKES.

Here, they sell 64-ounce Pepsi-Colas;
landscape is severe relief.
To ravage such a canyon,
even God must tire of level plain—
to split the earth this deep
for sulfur water, for gypsum.

Field Trip to Andrew Jackson's Hermitage, 1969

No sign of those who'd worked the house
or its kitchen, detached, to shield
the owners from its oppressive heat,
its crude tools like those of a livery.

No sign of those who'd worked the fields,
no quarters, cemetery or stones,
just some nameless grasses, burnt
but in the shade of a few massive oaks.

On the portico of the white-columned house
we waited out a belting rain, thunder
stampeding from behind the hills
like a herd of spooked horses.

Years later, they split open the field
to find a woman with a musket ball
lodged in her spine, shot as she was walking
or running away; a man's forearm,

as warped by hunger as a cane left out
in rain; and buried in the ash
of a forbidden campfire, a pig iron charm
forged in the shape of a fist.

Heirloom

My family doesn't save anything.
Perhaps we moved too often, or

had too little and plain wore it all
out. Once we owned chickens,

small store fronts, acres of fickle wheat.
Just outside the family plots, oil

rigs pumped day and night
making millions for their distant owners.

Homes we have lost: the first sod one
subsumed by plain; the next rickety

farmhouse got tired of leaning
into the wind.

This might explain our reverence,
immoderate, for what is left:

the single boot, the leather case
missing its spectacles, the photographs

whose subjects can no longer
be named. We try to reclaim,

as a circle of chairs recalls a gathering,
the curling yarn, its skein.

Dogwood Winter

Ravenous for horizon, young men used to climb
the town's fire tower and squint, trying to see
past the sparse lights, the river's bend, milky,
where the tannery pumped out lye.

A blight in the Ukraine tripled the price of corn
and the couple couldn't profit on hogs.
They bought peacocks after reading
they were easier to breed than chickens.
No one mentioned the racket the hens
made in season, how the Greeks heard
their tuneless caws as bad prophesy.

After the state flooded many good acres,
bevies of quail flocked into backyards,
and an old man known only as Hap
grabbed his gun, shot one, and two squirrels.

A boy was nicked and his mother
had to be taken to King's Lying-In.
Later the boy and two friends snuck back
into the old man's shed, stole
a six-point buck's caping from his ice chest.

Despite the consideration of lilies,
the consultation of almanacs,
and a wiry fig tree that had lucked through

the last three winters, the locals canned,
cured, and tithed. A deer could feed several,
meat fattened with suet. The skin sewn to hold
what they would call wine.

II. Selvage

On being mistaken for a whore in a laundromat, Pensacola, Florida, July 12, 1979

Luann in lotus position
on lime metal folding
chair, long blond hair
curling around her toes.
Me in tight waffle knit
top, strapless, sweating
over Sartre.

Maybe we should have cracked
your head with Luann's ten-pound
History of the Western World or
sacrificed my being and nothingness—
that which pleases the heart.

Maybe we should have
fucked you for broke, gone
out later for *dim sum.*

Maybe we should have
fucked you for broke, gone
out later for *dim sum.*

The Summer You Told Me I Was Beautiful

I must have believed you, because at the store
I passed over the chaste racers and maillots
and let my hand skim the bikini aisle's limes
and corals like an unmoored skiff on a bay.
And when I stepped out from behind
the white slatted doors, you told me how you loved
the slope of my belly from navel to pelvis,
the mole marking the narrows of my waist,
how the suit's bright triangles seemed to float
over my small breasts like flags on a still day.
Such a long time since I'd been with a man
who was willing to overlook the obvious.
I should have known if you would lie about this
you would about other things.

Einarsson

You did not tell me I was pretty.
You told me I was clean.

In bed, you ate slivers of cheese
off my stomach. Your fingernails
were the size of spoons.

Moving my legs into a new position,
your forehead beaded in an eagerness
I could not quite share. Although

I wanted to be a modern,
my best friend married
at sixteen. An old man

put down his whittling
and vouched for them. A clerk
gave them toothbrushes,

a bar of soap. All that,
to do what we are doing now.
You fish through a drawer,

hold up three black lace
panties, ask me to pick
which one is mine.

In the bathroom I find aspirin,
pour a glass of cold
water between my legs.

The signature on a postcard
stuck against the mirror ends
in "dottir." On the front,

an ocean the color of mercury,
two eider ducks daubed on
a skerry's shorefast ice.

Cinderella

She was tired of ash.
Of the filthiness of her neck.

This was her mistake—
to regard herself.

The barrel was filled with potatoes
for the following day's meal.

She picked one up and scrubbed,
its knobbed head callous as a priest's.

She scrubbed her fingers. Ragged nails,
pale moons and the singe beneath.

A mouse ran across the window,
its back stark in moonlight.

She took an ember in her skirt
and lit the fatwood.

When the muslin tablecloth went up,
she stepped into her molten slippers,

let the yellow finery of her hair
engulf the village.

Bell's Palsy

First I tasted what I thought to be Novocain,
but was instead the nerves of my tongue going dumb,
the burnt taste of circuits flickering, then gone.

The right side of my face went slack, not dead
(for the dead have their rigour).
My two halves provided sufficient contrast
to cause nudging and pointing in children.

Everyone gets a warning—a crunch in the chest,
a shortness of breath, the left arm going numb.
The body knows first, before the mind admits,

as when you can no longer stand your lover's
breath, and rush toward climax, grunt and shove
satisfactory nonetheless; why it's reasonable
for whores to charge more for kisses.

Paean to the Opiate

Bridegroom I'm true,
I'm bound—

dialing from a red booth,
brushing the door

of a stranger's sedan, cash
wet in my hand.

Light me dully in your pinhole eye.
Make me anew in your habit

of stunting, transient beauty—
irises growing more Delft.

You mute what's shrill, smelt
a face to its hallows.

I want you. I don't
need. Truly I need

less and less.
I can subsist in a room,

someone to fetch for me,
an almond, slice of orange,

Scheherazade, stuck,
scratching out the same track.

Déjeuner sur l'herbe

When I introduced him, you
were slouching on a shoddy tweed couch,

shot from years of students,
canvas sneaker dangling off a slim arch.

He kept asking me, tone nonchalant,
What's her name, the skinny one?

Now you, the ivory of you,
chaste black triangle,

and him, fully clothed, in rumpled
wool, oblique—

Why am I the one who's shamed,
backing away,

like a child from her parents' bed,
my face distorted in the brass knob

pudgy cheeks stretched fun-house
huge, mouth, a pink slit, and shut.

The More Dangerous Amusement

was what the obituary said after Nico
died riding her bicycle

more dangerous than
what?

you're supposed to have
another noun for comparison

I'm sure she owned a sports car or at least a Renault
or scooter to hug the twisting Ibizan roads

probably had her own works—
didn't need to share or steal the wrong kind from the clinic—

The nurse says my veins are better
I don't know, I'm thinking, better than

what? I need a noun   not euphoria,
not oblivion, but

Nico was German   not French like I'd thought
I'm not switching subjects because

it's a habit—smell like the bottom of a copper kettle
burnt from the time all the water boiled off   and the taste

caustic   like the lye that once splattered
my blouse in high school chemistry—

I thought I had cleaned it all off
but later

it left marks
in all the places it had touched

Chew

They snare me in leather
like something least and feral.
Haven't they noticed
I can't lift a fork?

I was once philosophical.
Snagged some scissors
from the nurse's station.
Locked the stall and worked over
the pales of a forearm.
Now they don't let me
near anything interesting.

The old nurse squats at my bed,
her face grave, as if she's been called
to pass down some essential skill
to the last idiot female of the clan—

this is how we make paiwari, soften leather—

and when I won't, she pries
the hole open with the spoon—

Liver's Retort

Don't fret. I can go for years on spite.
Sure, your joints ache a bit, friends say
you're more forgetful,
but aren't I the one organ
that can regenerate itself?

Still, I'm no martyr; I've kept track—
the way you clogged my portal artery,
pocked my flesh necrotic,
savoring what was my demise—

the sweet-sour smell of mash,
the pop its caramel-colored trickle made
as it cracked neat chinks of ice—
the days you still bothered
to drink from a glass.

She Dreams of Four Ways Around Her Dilemma

> *. . . and both seemed secure—*
> *She in her virtue, he in his hauteur*
> —from *Don Juan, Canto 13*

1.
One hundred degrees. How can you resist me,
a pool of water cooling under elms?
You dive in. Liquid, I envelop you,
can feel all your body at once—jaw's stubble,
sheath of chest muscles, navel's quick indentation.
Then you stand up, splashing onto the grass.
I bead, dripping from your back and neck;
blue is the color of regret.

2.
My body becomes chador; my skin
drapes in loose dark folds.
Only my eyes visible: they adore you.
Though even they wear dark glasses.

3.
You are an immortal. Bored,
you visit me and other women.
Afterwards, I float, I'm a lily,
I'm a waterfowl.
Over a cigarette, you do a fine job
of refuting the concept of free will.

4.
I am a lady, and you, my dark gentleman.
I write you sonnets. Each one I crumple
into small rounds that become dark pearls.
When finished, I am old. I bathe in pearls.
I do not remember you, grain of sand in the center.

Other Means Having Failed

To recall that last winter requires a grim conjuring:
how I tread the cheap rug waiting,
how you kept a prescription on the nightstand
so that when you came home,
you could still be gone.
But these words tell nothing about you.
As I say them, I see you go up the flue,
a ghost of soot. I could mention your gait—
like a marionette's, childlike and inhabited;
your habit of tamping a filtered cigarette.
I believe you knew I was still in the room:
sun nodding into early twilight,
as if it were something we shared.

Ritual

before candor and therefore
a lull coated our tongues like fur
skin smelling of sweat and camphor

the sign said not to get close
to the crumbling ledge
where wire fencing had worn

the scrub near the mouth
appeared pillowed   verdant
we lay down the mat
took turns feeling
the other's weight
a rare coolness expelled
from the deep well

I had thought you might notice the shift
small rocks tumbling over the edge
the smell suddenly sulfurous

You were buying *salbutes*
from a makeshift stand
when the guide told me

this is the place
children were sacrificed

thrown into the *cenote's*
deep and jeweled blue

Selvage

After weeks on interferon,
I start taking an undue interest
in my own slough: clumps of hair,
scales that fall from my scalp,
fine as talc, powdering the bathroom floor.

I don't know. Maybe I think
I can put it all back. I buy
some tar lotion, some oil
to slather on at night
under a bathing cap.

I lock myself in the bathroom,
run water from the tap each time
I need to give myself a shot
so the children don't notice.

Meanwhile, I wallow in it:
one major organ, compromised,
yellowing; flu-like symptoms,
nonexistent thyroid, membranes
drying up like rills after the spring.
The havoc downstream.

Viral count rebounds, a healthy jolt
of yourowndamnfault. The nurse
who draws blood confirms

with one sharp look at my chart,
the pop of her latex gloves.

You should know better—
what Grandmother might say.
Know ye not that ye are the temple.
I know my New Testament.

I know—
even selvage
can be tucked under for a hem, a seam,
if you need to make allowances.
Hidden there, dense as nuclei,
a dot for each color of the cloth,
visible only if rent.

III. Passional

Peine forte et dure

Sometimes you want horrible things to happen.
During a lightning storm you say to yourself:
Let me be the rod that culminates a striking.

You're feeling clever, testing out a bit of reverse
psychology on God like you try with your children:
I'll bet you can't be quiet for a whole minute.

And it's not at all like this, you learn—after
you've held someone in your arms
(my son, breathless and curled, perfect feet still warm)—

and felt the heaviness descend, as if you were the accused
pressed under the boards, when you say to yourself
If I wake, I must make a good of this,

Or afterwards, when, rock by rock, you are lightened,
the gauze removed from your eyes.
The names of things return: bootlace,

postcard, the precision of sounds:
schoolyard bells, a choir of child voices
gathering under a canopy of elms.

Che gelida manina

Over my door they put a blue heart
to alert the nurses and orderlies. Still,
a nurse asks about the baby, then
reddening, makes a note on my chart.

We dress you in a christening gown,
gold-plated cross
Grandmother bought in Matamoras.
Into the hem I thread blue ribbon.

The cousin who is four months along
tells me she likes the name Benjamin.
She suggests I use it again
if we have another son.

Gladioli overpower the fiberglass casket.
They no longer offer pine.
That your finger would curl around mine
they term an automatic reflex.

Cave

He wouldn't get stuck down here.
There are always two possibilities:
construct or deconstruct.

He takes plastic tubing, plumbs wells
in the backyards of companies
looks for heavy metals, PCBs.
He doesn't despair, but charts their plumes
on green paper, notes his findings
like a Victorian naturalist.

He can eat the same sandwich for lunch for a year.
A little routine might help,
a remark he reserves
for when he believes I've exhausted all reason.
How do I explain?
It presupposes an order, and I see, if I see,

something like a supermarket,
with dark and flooded aisles,
and I don't have too much time so I
grab everything—stalagmites, books,
pieces of string, cartons and cartons
of Gretel's cookies.

I might not have arrived at the right conclusion.

All night I rip open box after box,
devour each sweet morsel to a crumb.
I can't tell—
all I'm left with is an aftertaste of metal or
gunpowder, the silhouettes of gods
formed in the flickering light
before dispersing wildly overhead.

The Plot in North Village

Trees live comfortably among their dead.
Staunch elm and maple sapling stand
next to the fallen, bark
scalloped with fungus.

Last week, the neighbor's mare foaled—
her colt starved in a day. Yet she stamped
and broke for us when we tried
to take him away.

In Lancaster, you lie under a stone
dated with a single year. My son,
will we reunite here, in this darker,

infinite womb:
hair slack as rain, fingers curled,
brains two harps strummed then quiet,
eyes neither seeing nor blind?

Anniversary

I. Other Women

It happened a year ago.
I began to age in a noticeable way.
Veins appeared inside my knees:
fine red lines like the ones on maps
that mark unimportant boundaries.
Other women do not grow old.
The blonde, who I often follow
when I exit the commuter train,
is as tall and sturdy as a poplar.
Her creamy feet, in Roman sandals
with stacked brown heels,
make me weep.

II. Sing, Nightingale

Who would think of leaving
the white colonial possessing
authentic hinged shutters,
still useful against a storm.
With its front door flung,
the staircase, red carpeted
by the moving company,
is an open gullet, astounded
as Philomela that it has
no more stories to tell.

III. Revelation

The elderly couple from Sicily courted
in the old way. On their wedding night
she was most disturbed when he removed
his hat. She had never seen him without it.
I embarrass you now, in that same way.
Taking off what I thought did not matter,
taking off a little of me—stranger,
and stranger still.

Promise, No Pinky Cross

Dear friend, I don't want to trust, either.

A girlfriend returned my favorite dress
permanently stained with barbeque sauce.
When I defended my brother's D+ in calculus,
my father turned and said that at least he
wasn't studying something meaningless.
My old beau gave me the turquoise ring
his other girlfriend thought looked cheap.

Your left leg's restless pumping
threatened to tip the café table
as our talk approached an intimacy.
You kept trying to spear the same limp carrot
and missing. If I were a lady,
and carried a compact with loose powder,
I might have spotted my own peculiar
fidgets—hair twirling, lip licking.

I cannot promise you that kind of sweet
and absolute confidence we would have had as girls
when your best friend was assigned
to the desk in front of you, alphabetically.

Here are my car keys, a long list of subjects
about which I know nothing,
and my Grandmother's recipe for Red Devil's Food Cake
with her note, *Vinegar is what makes it.*

I have no ideas, but I do have some things

I have baby poo under my nails, diaper pail that the dog always gets into.
I have coo and a pastel giraffe that plays Tchaikovsky.

I have green bean casserole with a pre-fried onion ring topping.
I have homework, common cold.
I have muddling over Modern French Novel.
I have bookmark that invariably goes missing.

I have *What the hell?*
I have *Just pick up where you left off.*
I have children who claim they won't read
when they're grown and don't have to.

I have an invisible sign that says interrupt me
if I don't appear to be giving you my undivided attention
or if I try to engage myself in a conversation
that might involve ideas, even a simpleton's idea of ideas,
such as why the latest star vehicle went straight to video.

I have unashamed displays of love showered upon me
undeservedly and in their own sweet time, in the way that
very complex natural phenomena have dubious theories as to their cause
but consistent and demonstrable effects.

I have a dailiness dissolved into more or less endless variations
on the same domestic themes, which when captured on home video
depict a woman with thinner hair and thicker waist
than the person formerly known as "myself" who I once believed
to hold some sway over her own, albeit small, universe.

And I have lack of concentration to a sublime—
words woozling in front of my eyes like drunks
who stagger out of a party long after
their so-called welcome has worn off
and hit them like a barn door in the back—
who had been quite entertaining before they turned belligerent,
railing on as if they had to for their very survival.

Kneeling Under Sky, Against Which, The Clouds

In the cold bed, knees curl fetal to chest—
my limbs know to preserve themselves.
My mouth—pink rag of tongue
swabbing every inch of gum
to dislodge a single seed.

Yet while my brainstem stokes,
sweat, breathe, shit,
and my occipital lobe reviews
the figures exiting the train
to find the one familiar,

something else wants dissolution:
to veer toward orchard's stone wall,
where apple trees stipple
the lovely morning sun.

Ya Muhyi, Ya Mumit—
do you desire equally to manifest in me
as in yet unwritten scores,
marble cliffs dissolved to karst,
the pinhole of a vanished star?

Cosmology

His mother fed him at specified intervals.
And when nothing would stop him
from sucking his fingers,
she taped three of them together,
then four, and finally even the thumb.

Unable to comfort himself,
he screamed, even after his mother
stilled the mobile of songbirds,
pulled the green shades,
dissolving their fluttering shapes.

Years later a lover would discover
the flat spot on the back of his head.
Hours spent lying in a crib.

He doesn't believe in reductionism,
he tells her, or the significance of the dream
in which he flails off the edge of the bed
like a ship into the swirl of demons
depicted in archaic maps of the world.

Subtext of the Latest Rejection

Dear Miss Poetess, we regret ... but
your references seem dated.
Even if you were the first little girl
in your class to read, something
clearly went wrong.
What happened to your pursuit
of the existential novel?
What happened to Jacques Lacan?

Last spotted you were nose-deep
in a celebrity magazine.
You say the stories remind you
of the Greeks'—demi-gods
with exaggerated personality flaws,
but then, why so much time
ogling pectorals and derrieres?

You never were one of us.
Your ode to the most recently rediscovered
Roman poet came a bit too late.
You still mangle Mr. Roethke's
sir name and Mr. Heaney's
Christian one. Perhaps

you missed your calling,
as it's a marvel how prolific
you can wax over how
to get out a blood stain,
the smell of cat
from a mattress.

Aim, lower. Better,
try the scatter approach.
Eventually,
something will hit.

Michelangelo's Eves

Creation

The Man is asleep. The Woman is pleading with God
to stay born. God still seems to be considering
whether this species would be simpler male,
rid of blood, milk, and afterbirth,
the randomness of meiosis replaced by cloning.

Temptation

It is hard to tell what she is. She is clearly
derivative, muscular, with torso thick
enough to house his ribs.
And as she reaches for the fruit
her biceps bulge above breast buds,
sex camouflaged. Adam is reaching
above her head toward the other Eve
who has the same Etruscan face,
same red hair, but whose sex
has morphed into a flesh-colored
snake, coiled around the tree.

Expulsion

Michelangelo considered his sketches inferior
to the final paintings and wanted them destroyed.
In the preliminary drawing, Eve's arms encircle
her body. Her head down, one hand raised,
any alarm in her face hidden, her defense
self-contained. Not like the woman painted
on the ceiling: body crouched, face raw
with terror, looking back over her shoulder
for Adam to save her.

Antiphon

Light that should bring light hobbles—
my body, its smell of sour cabbage,
and my mind, already twitching for pills
to embalm with the blackness
of a new moon.

My daughter listens
at the bottom of the stairs
like a shepherdess attuned to the bells
of goats that lack the good sense
to walk down the slope
of the riverbank to drink.

From there the damped notes come,
a clear moving stream across shale,
vowels of my name.

Locus

I want to run away from home
like the famous Chinese chef
whose whereabouts foodies pursue relentlessly
on the Internet

He takes his wife with him
two framed photos of cooking awards
which he nails to the walls of the new restaurant

He must not own a house
If he did he could not move so stealthily
leaving only speculation for months
until someone finds him making
spicy cumin-scented whole fish in Richmond

He must not have children
Children do not like to be moved
their feet like stumps their fingers like roots

Maybe they are more like the original peoples
smell their ancestors in the dirt

And the very young protest
in the way that boxes do   becoming
unwieldy   heavy

You must sling them around your waist
balance them on a hip and be prepared
to drag so many things along with them

    bottles   nipples   thermometers   cradles
that can't be stacked like packages
of bean curd or noodles   spices
labeled with their country of origin

Lazarus

One of the paid mourners
spilt wine onto my face.
Under the shroud my mouth parted
like some simple creature's—
liquid dribbling out,
stiffening constrictions of gauze.

I want it to have happened
in the way I was told,
not how I remember:
stench and myrrh, heavy rust
of my tongue, although
for a time, I was no longer brother
to anyone, more akin to the dust
that glints and is lost in sand
on mornings the women beat their rugs.

Cassandra at Dinner

Broadside bumping the swinging door,
she's doing the nightly kowtow out of the kitchen,
trying to lighten her husband's sour demeanor,
shucking, jiving, fingers gripping a cold plate,
thumb mired in a piece of gristly roast
someone had chewed and spit back out.
Bent over the sink, she scrapes
off the indifference of her youngest
to the latest à la carte, whitish bread smeared
with whiter fluff, quartered, crusts cut off.
It's just in her nature, she tells herself, the way she feels
more comfortable serving. She wasn't forced,
stolen, sold for sheer loveliness. She has credit,
place settings for twelve, and a seer's curse:
to see her future, more or less,
lack the gumption to alter it.

Relations

The gold heads of chrysanthemums
bend toward the casement window.
Their stems discolor the vase water;
their smell hangs like vinegar in the air.

Bent near the casement window
their mother lies, her skin oyster white.
The smell of food trays hangs in the air.
She doesn't seem to know they're there.

She lied about the oyster-white mints.
She never touched them.
She doesn't seem to know they're there.
Outside, rain mats the leaves of yellow maples.

Her children no longer touch her.
They watch TV, switch to a game show.
Outside, yellow maples, matted by rain,
appear like an abstraction of chrysanthemums.

They switch to a game show from the Christian channel.
Head bent, she doesn't notice the gold
of the chrysanthemums, the room's sour smell,
the restless sons who take turns guessing.

Anniversary

I can explain the way your skin
smells in summer, can trace
the whorls of hair on your crown,
can hear the slight inhalation
that is all that remains of a stutter.

Stars and mandolins, canteens
of wine, brown bread wrapped
in twine and paper—
I was careless, but now I will barter
with the days for you.

Before it is bare, the gingko
will perfect the color yellow.
Across the road,
a car backs out of the drive,
and for a while, the dog's head
stays even with the accelerating wheels.

Passional

The farm road ends in a field
of last year's wheat, mangled
by combines, blanched by ice.
Beyond the clearing, a trail
grazed by now-starved deer,
trees stripped of bark at eye level.
I regret I cannot speak to him
who has no words; bear to touch
the sleeves of his carelessness.
I had to tell my children something.
I took them to the torn spot
in the fence where chicken wire curled,
stretched it between posts
and fastened it there.

Bee Balm

You arrive in June in bergamot frock
and for two weeks a shocking pink bejewels
your head—coronation of homely stalk,
the fluffed topknot of a starlet's poodle.
Next to foxglove's smooth and dappled orchid,
your tinted Mohawk looks disheveled, punk.
If rose is pure scarlet ego; you're id,
minty leaves seeking unabated sun.
You were an afterthought—easy grower—
not adored like my black-hearted poppies.
The hummingbird stops darting to hover
slowly, mesmerized by your nectaries,
as if it knows its beak's narrow lumen
can admit such pleasure only in drams.

From stars

we are made and they us—
carbon to carbon, hydrogen to hydrogen.

Must I choose which
universe—bound or eternal—

    with the certainty

that Spring will come again?
Through the snow cover

I can imagine leaf and sepal
trillium, clover, cinquefoil,

in April, and in June, clusters
of frog eggs coupled to a rotting log—

So when I mean to say
I love you

    twenty years having
    passed

as we draw close—

I say

Yes,

this is the one, dear,

this park, this park bench.

The Child in Wonder Falling on Grass

Spring's early heat turns you to dervish.
Your knees soiled green from tumbles,
with wild screams you protest mother's firm grip.
Then, minutes later you sleep, curled in her lap.
Smells of coming rain, mud, and wild onion
surround you, while farther, only inches
in the great scheme, expands the black unbreatheable,
which astronauts say smells like burning tungsten.
This year, the black drop of Venus will mar
the perfect sphere of our small dense star.
A middling yellow one among millions similar,
it warms your skin, the grass, the dirt below the grass,
as it absorbs the remnants of supernovas
bursting their whipped cores.

Notes

Tennessee Walker, "Tennessee Walker." Shorthand for Tennessee Walking horse, a breed of pleasure horse, known for its calm temperament and comfortable riding gait.

Peine forte et dure, "Peine forte et dure."(*Fr.* Pain, hard and long) A form of torture used during the Salem Witch trials in which a person is placed under planks, and heavy rocks are applied in order to induce a confession or death, or both.

Che gelida menina, "Che gelida menina."(*It.* What a cold little hand!) Aria from Puccini's *La Boheme*.

Ya Muhyi, Ya Mumit, "Kneeling Under Sky, Against Which, The Clouds." (Arabic) Among the 99 Beautiful Names of Allah are *Ya Muhyi*, "Giver of Life," and *Ya Mumit*, "Taker of Life."